# Introduction

Welcome to **Art Store 2**, a five-part unit in **The Mix**, the Channel 4 Schools arts series for 7–11 year olds.

These programmes illustrate how art can be prompted by observing the world around us. Our environment, full of natural and made objects, people and places, is the source of inspiration and the starting point for most artistic practice. All artists learn to look closely at their environment, to record it, analyse it, and transform it in their work.

The emphasis in these five programmes is on taking the time really to look at the world and see with fresh eyes all the things that usually pass us by. This central idea of close observation is captured in the sketchbook entries of the presenter as she introduces each topic: the line and tone of ordinary objects; the patterns on seashells and paving in a street; the simple textures in everyday materials; the immediate worlds of colour and structure.

There is not just one 'correct' way of approaching art and there are as many ways of looking at something as there are artists. As each programme explores a different element, the presenter, artist Jo Volley, demonstrates how she approaches a piece of artwork. This encourages play and exploration, an openness to ideas and the freedom to experiment with similar techniques in the primary classroom.

We hope that you enjoy the programmes and that the children find them stimulating. We are always pleased to receive feedback about the programmes and the accompanying support materials as well as any examples of children's work.

Adrienne Jones
Education Officer
Channel 4 Schools
PO Box 100
Warwick
CV34 6TZ

## contents

⟩ This **Channel 4 Schools** series is subtitled on page 888 of Teletext for the deaf and hearing-impaired.

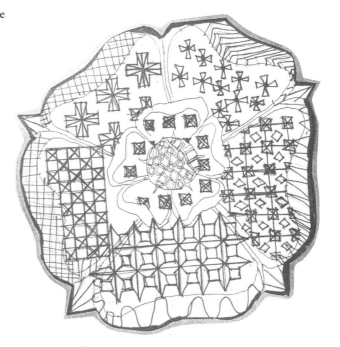

# Art Store 2 and the curriculum

## The programmes

The **Art Store 2** programmes provide a stimulating and comprehensible introduction to art education which embraces the curriculum targets for Art & Design in England, Wales and Northern Ireland and the Expressive Arts curriculum in Scotland.

Artists have always been inspired by their environment and use it as a starting point for all manner of work. Each programme in this unit uses the environment as a focus for illustrating a chosen theme and a particular skill. **Art Store 2** aims to develop understanding of the basic elements of art – line, tone, shape, colour, pattern, texture and structure – through observational work 'on location' at the supermarket, the park, the home, the market and the seaside.

By using a sketchbook as a visual diary in which to record from observation in these five different locations, the presenter makes drawings and collects interesting and accessible items to use back in her studio. By her examples of different skills and techniques, children are shown how to work in a variety of media which includes drawing, painting, printmaking, collage and sculpture.

The unit highlights the processes used by artists. As the presenter develops her work she 'thinks aloud', externalising the process of art through constant engagement with it.

## The Teachers' Guide

**Art Store 2** aims to help non-specialist primary teachers to teach art. This Guide shows how projects develop through a gradual progression of skills and ideas, with each stage evolving from the previous one. Integral to this process are the qualities of different media, the skills in handling basic materials, and the importance of experimenting with tools and materials.

## Resource collections

The Guide emphasises the importance of resources. Teachers are encouraged to build up their own class collections. Teachers should identify the differences between manufactured and natural forms in these collections, which can be both a focus and a trigger when developing schemes of work for art.

## Pupil resource sheets

These photocopiable pages are intended to help pupils with their sketchbook activities. Each one is based on the programme content and gives ideas and suggested activities to help pupils with their own work. Sometimes children are daunted by blank pages in a sketchbook, so there are activities which suggest that they collect flat items such as labels, stamps, and photographs that interest them, to use in a collage on one of the pages of their sketchbook. This is a good way for the children to make the sketchbook their own: a journal to which they will want to add.

## The language of art

Art provides a wealth of language opportunities. **Art Store 2** offers a starting point for developing imaginative vocabulary, questions and answers. Art can help develop speaking, listening, writing and reading skills as it provides rich stimuli and varied contexts for the development of language. Through first-hand observation of the environment, imagination, diverse ways to express ideas and feelings, and the use of tools, materials and techniques, art activities offer great potential for developing vocabulary.

## Organisation

Depending on the way in which art is incorporated in the curriculum, the activities suggested in this Guide can be carried out with either the whole class or groups of children working independently.

# The programmes

| Programmes | Content | Art outcomes |
|---|---|---|
| **1. Line:** Drawing | • Using the local environment (the supermarket) as a stimulus for developing observation and artwork.<br>• Using sketchbooks to collect visual information.<br>• Exploring different kinds of line and shape.<br>• Experimenting with a range of pencils to create tonal shading to show form.<br>• How to arrange, plan out and draw a still-life composition.<br>• Looking at the drawings of artists.<br>• Vocabulary related to line. | • Developing sketchbook skills.<br>• Developing knowledge, understanding and skills using line, shape and tone.<br>• Experimenting with drawing tools and materials to make marks and tones.<br>• Understanding form, perspective and composition.<br>• Finding out about the work of artists and the processes used.<br>• Developing appropriate art vocabulary. |
| **2. Colour:** Painting | • Using the local environment, for example the park, to explore colours.<br>• How to experiment with primary and secondary colour mixing.<br>• Experimenting with a range of paint brushes.<br>• Developing a colour palette and naming colours.<br>• Creating tints and shades, complementary and harmonious colours.<br>• Planning backgrounds and completing a still-life painting of flowers.<br>• Vocabulary related to colour. | • Knowledge and understanding of colour theory and colour mixing.<br>• Setting up and organising a paint area.<br>• Understanding that colours can express feelings, such as the response to warm and cold colours.<br>• Appreciating colour in the environment, for example flowers in the park.<br>• Pupils' evaluation of their own work. Modifying and adapting paintings. Expressing preferences and opinions.<br>• Learning about the colour work of artists.<br>• Developing appropriate art vocabulary. |
| **3. Pattern:** Printing | • Patterns in the natural and made environments.<br>• Experimenting with pattern-making.<br>• Printing onto fabric using relief blocks.<br>• Regular and irregular shapes.<br>• Observing forms and textures of shells, pebbles and seaweed.<br>• Vocabulary related to pattern. | • Appreciation and knowledge of pattern in the natural and made worlds.<br>• Sketchbook work.<br>• Understanding how patterns can be created by drawing, printing and stencilling.<br>• Pattern-making using relief printing.<br>• Planning and predicting repeat pattern sequences.<br>• Understanding how artists and designers use patterns to develop designs and abstract work.<br>• Organisation of tools, materials and equipment.<br>• Collaborating with others, expressing preferences and opinions.<br>• Developing pattern-related vocabulary. |
| **4. Texture:** Collage | • Responses to textures in the different rooms in the house, and in the garden.<br>• Making textures through paint and rubbings.<br>• How to make a texture collage.<br>• The qualities of materials – plastic, wood, metal, textiles, etc.<br>• Vocabulary related to texture. | • Understanding and appreciation of tactile and sensory responses.<br>• Exploring and experimenting with textures in a variety of ways.<br>• Understanding the properties and textures of a range of different materials – wood, metal, plastic, etc.<br>• How different materials are used by artists, sculptors and designers.<br>• Developing appropriate art vocabulary. |
| **5. Structure:** 3-D modelling | • Using the local environment to explore structure and three dimensions.<br>• Using fruit as a stimulus for three-dimensional work.<br>• Making a structure using withies and tissue paper.<br>• Scale: how to enlarge.<br>• Using a sketchbook to plan ideas.<br>• Vocabulary related to structure and form. | • Understanding form and space using natural and made artefacts.<br>• Making structures and creating work in three dimensions.<br>• Showing three dimensions on a two-dimensional surface using drawing and shading.<br>• Using a sketchbook to collect information, plan ideas and record the working process.<br>• Organising the art area for successful three-dimensional work.<br>• Discussing work as it progresses. Solving problems as they occur.<br>• Developing appropriate art vocabulary. |

# 1 | Line

## Programme outline

Ideas for drawing interesting shapes can be found in all sorts of places. We meet Jo, the presenter, in her local supermarket, where she explains that drawing is about ways of looking at objects, practising sketching them, and then making line drawings. We look at the shape of different items, the idea of simple perspective, composition and tone (the way light falls on an object to create shadows and depth).

In her studio, Jo demonstrates some practical aspects of drawing which include: different types of pencil and the lines they produce; how to hold a pencil; how to draw lines; how tone is used to shade and how it is graduated to create the effect of three dimensions. A sequence showing the work of children reflects these skills.

Finally, we see some work from other artists who have drawn still life. These include Giorgio Morandi, Braque and Alberto Giacometti.

## Learning outcomes

The children should gain an understanding of:

- Drawing for different purposes: to describe, record, analyse, investigate, communicate messages, tell stories, express feelings and ideas.

- How to use drawing tools to record observations.

- How a sketchbook can be used to collect information, explore marks and practise drawing skills.

- How to show three dimensions by using pencil shading to create forms.

- The process used by artists to select, collect and develop artwork – in this case, drawing.

## Key concepts...

Observation, still life, 2-D, 3-D, line, tone, shape, form, light, dark, shadow, cross-hatching, shading, contrast, viewpoint, viewfinder, perspective.

## ...and vocabulary

Background, foreground, near, far, outline, position, placement, composition, names of shapes (ellipse, cylinder, cube, sphere), measurement (dimension, scale, width, length, breadth).

## Helpful resources: about drawing

- Examples of drawings made for different purposes, such as illustrations, maps, diagrams, architectural drawings, cartoons (examples from prints and books); from different periods (cave drawings); representing world cultures; drawings in different media (pencil, chalk, charcoal, pastel, pen, ink, coloured pencils); viewfinders and magnifying glasses; a variety of packaging and shopping, including vegetables of different shapes and sizes, and labels from home or the supermarket.

## Before viewing

▶ With the whole class, look at still-life drawings and paintings by two or three artists. Ask the children to make a list of the artefacts or objects within them.

▶ Encourage the children to collect shopping items or packages. Discuss shape and form and ask the children to record the names in their sketchbooks.

▶ Help the children to make a list of key words related to drawing for display in the classroom.

## Whilst viewing

▶ The children could be asked:

- What artefacts have been chosen for the still-life composition?

## After viewing

### Plan a still-life drawing with the class

▶ Find out what the children know about drawing. For example: Who draws? What kinds of drawings are there? What drawing tools can be used? Discuss the aims of the work, which are to develop the children's observational skills and drawing techniques.

## Materials and equipment

Drawing tools such as graphite sticks, charcoal, wax crayons, pastels, pens and biros, brushes, rubbers and rulers (for occasional use), pencils for sketching (hard HB and softer 2B or 6B), sketchbooks, and a 'drawing outside' wallet – comprising pencils, felt pens, rubber, small viewfinder, pencil sharpener and clipboard to lean on, and drawing paper, cartridge or good newsprint paper.

## Prepare drawing tools and materials

▶ Talk about the variety of drawing tools – hard pencils for close observational work, chalks or charcoal for bolder work. Ask the children to use their sketchbook to explore a range of these drawing tools, making a note of each one as it creates a different effect. Encourage the children to hold the pencil in different ways: loosely between the fingers, gripping tightly at the top, or in the palm of the hand.

## Exploring different lines

▶ Set the class a challenge to find and describe nine different kinds of line in the classroom and record these in their sketchbooks. Ask them to divide their paper into nine squares and to draw different kinds of line in each square: for example, curvy, crinkly, zig-zag, wavy, fat, thin, parallel, circular, gentle and hard, using contrasting pressures and making corners, angles and lines that spiral. They can draw the line, describe it in words and note where it was seen.

## Exploring different shapes and tones

▶ Talk about shapes in the classroom. Ask the children to draw and name them in their sketchbooks. Make a word list to display: for example, square, circle, triangle, oblong, oval, regular and irregular shapes, pear-shaped and bottle-shaped outlines. Talk about three-dimensional forms and show the class some examples: cube, cylinder, sphere, cone, pyramid. Ask the children to record these words in their sketchbook. Demonstrate drawing a shape and shading around it to give a three-dimensional impression. Ask the children to practise their shading techniques using one or two shapes.

## Shading

▶ Shading is used to emphasise light and dark areas in a drawing and is often used to create a mood or feeling. Talk to the class about light and dark areas in the classroom and where the light is falling. Ask them to divide a piece of paper into boxes and practise holding the pencil loosely between the fingers and flat to the paper using the side of the lead – pressing gently at first, then increasing the pressure to gradate the tone from light to dark across the squares to end up with a dark square.

## Cross-hatching

▶ Cross-hatching is another way to create dark and light tones. The darker areas are made by adding more overlapping lines. Ask the children to divide their paper into squares again and this time to hold their pencil more firmly and upright so that they are using the pencil point to make a series of light-to-dark boxes using cross-hatched lines.

They could try a range of different pens and pencils, experimenting with spacing between the lines, different pressures, curved and straight lines, tightly arranged and more random ones, fast and slow lines.

## Using a sketchbook – a visual diary

▶ Talk to the class about the many purposes of a sketchbook and how important they are to artists. In the programme, we see how the artist uses her sketchbook: to work outside, to record ideas, to collect interesting things, to experiment with tools and materials, to keep an ongoing record of work, to make notes and record new vocabulary.

To develop the children's observation and confidence in using a sketchbook:

● Ask them to select one natural and one made object and make drawings of them in their sketchbooks. Suggest that they draw in the middle of the paper to give themselves plenty of room.

- Get them to practise drawing objects quickly. Give them a time limit, or ask them to keep a record of how long each drawing takes.

- Encourage them to use viewfinders to help focus down and select particular parts of the objects.

- Ask them to practise drawing the same object from different viewpoints.

- Remind them to annotate and to date all their work.

## Setting up a still life

In the programme we see the artist making choices and deciding what to include in her still life. Before the children make their own still-life drawings they will need some help in choosing and setting up the objects. They will need to be reminded not to sit too near to the table or easel. They need to be able to move their wrist easily.

▶ Before beginning, ask them to 'warm up' by practising drawing circles, ellipses and cubes in their sketchbooks.

**Step 1** Discuss the possible still-life items with the class. Encourage the selection of things that could be used: a packet, a bottle, something natural, like fruit.

**Step 2** Talk about whether the most appropriate way round for the paper is portrait or landscape. The children can then mark up their paper by dividing it into four equal squares using lightly drawn pencil lines.

**Step 3** Remind them to squint their eyes to see the main forms, the tones, the direction of the light and the shadows. When the objects have been selected and arranged, and before beginning the drawing, ask the children to walk around the composition, looking at it through a viewfinder and sketching it quickly from two different viewpoints. Remind them about shape, form and line.

**Step 4** The children now sketch each object in place and use their pencil shading to show the forms and textures.

**Key points to remind the children about when drawing:**

- Try not to use your rubber too much!

- Keep checking the spaces between the objects.

- Leave the detail until the end.

- Continuously ask yourself questions about what you're doing.

- Where is it darkest/ lightest/ longest/ thinnest?

- How wide is the base compared with the top?

- How much does it curve?

- Let your eyes travel up and down – not your head.

**Step 5** When the children have completed their drawings, ask them to view them from a short distance away. Encourage them to speak about what they think of their work, what they have learnt and what they might remember when they make another drawing. Display the drawings together with the vocabulary the children have learnt or used throughout the work.

## Collage drawing

▶ The still life in the programme was inspired by items from a supermarket. As a follow-up activity, with a focus on shape and lettering, ask the class to use packaging and labels from the class collection to make an interesting collage.

▶ Some of the packaging could be unfolded to discover the net shapes and, together with the food labels, overlapped in a collage. The children could use a viewfinder to choose a section from the collage and to draw this detail in their sketchbooks. When they have made a line drawing of their chosen section, ask them to practise shading the dark and light areas using pencils or to try another section of the collage, this time using coloured pencils.

## The language of art

The **sketchbook activity** on page 7 asks children to communicate graphically and substitute pictures for words.

▶ Give out the sheet for the children to complete.

# Sketchbook activity

▶ In your sketchbook, make up your own shopping list, but instead of using words, draw each item you want to buy.

Start off with the words: 'This week I need...' or 'My favourite shopping items are...'

▶ Design your own carrier bag to carry the shopping home. Include, in your design, drawings of some of the things you have bought.

▶ Draw the carrier bag to show what it looks like. Remember to add shading.

SCHOOLS

# 2 Colour

## Programme outline

A walk in the park is the starting point for this programme which is all about colour. The flowers in full bloom present an opportunity to explore the 'science of colour' – to identify primary and secondary colours, warm and cold colours, complementary colours and harmonising colours.

We look at how colour alters according to different light, and at tone, and at the language of colour. We begin to think about how colour makes us feel. Why, for example, are there so many bright reds and golds?

The presenter covers the following points in her practical demonstration in the studio as she paints a colourful still life: choosing brushes, paint and paper, the basic colour palette, warm colours and cold colours, mixing primary colours to make secondary shades, lightening or darkening the tone; how to 'frame' and paint a still-life composition step by step. A class of children is shown mirroring this work.

Finally, we see some works by other artists who have painted flowers. These include: Juan de Arellano's *Basket with Flowers*, Henri Rousseau's *Bouquet of Flowers*, Vincent Van Gogh's *Irises*.

## Learning outcomes

The children should gain an understanding of:

- How to observe and appreciate colours in their surroundings.

- The colour wheel.

- How to explore and experiment with colour mixing using primary colours.

- How to choose appropriate brushes and paper.

- How to plan and paint a composition.

- How to modify and adapt their work as it develops.

- Appropriate art vocabulary associated with painting.

- How some artists work.

## Key concepts...

Colour wheel, impasto (use of thick paint), sgraffito (scratching into surface), hue (the quality of a colour), intensity (the strength and brilliance of a colour), tone (the depth of a colour between the two extremes of black and white), monochrome (colours in the same tonal range).

## ...and vocabulary

Portrait, background, middle ground, foreground, harmonious, warm, cool, tint, shade, intense, opaque, transparent, reflect, pigments, contrast, technique, effect, subtle, consistency, wash. Names of colours such as vermilion, scarlet, Prussian blue, magenta, cyan, chrome.

## Helpful resources: relating to paint

Collect examples of paintings showing intense colour work.

- Commercial paint colour charts, examples of artists' work with a strong focus on colour, flower paintings, viewfinders and magnifying glasses, a range of (primary) coloured papers, threads, materials, and flowers.

Prepare a chart to show the varied marks that brushes can make.

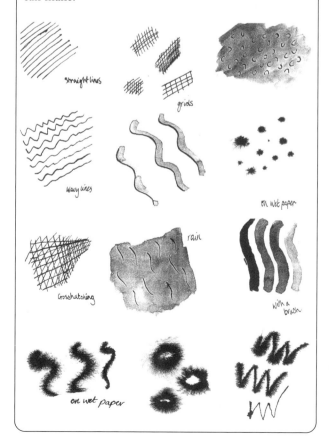

straight lines

grids

wavy lines

on wet paper

rain

crosshatching

with a brush

on wet paper

# Before viewing

▶ Find out what the children understand and know about colour and painting.

▶ Take the class for a walk in the park, with sketchbooks, to record colours.

▶ Make a list of key vocabulary related to colour and painting for display in the classroom.

▶ Talk to the children about the best layout and organisation of the painting area.

# Whilst viewing

▶ The children could be asked:

● To name some of the colours seen in the programme so far.

● What colours the artist has mixed to get a particular colour.

● What would happen if she added a bit more red or yellow.

# After viewing
## Plan a painting project with the class

▶ Introduce the work by looking at paintings and talking about colours. Talk about the aims of the project: to develop their knowledge, understanding and skills in colour mixing and painting. Emphasise that much of the work will be about exploring and experimenting with paints and colours as well as making a painting. Look at different kinds of paint: powder paints, ready-mixed paint, acrylic, oils, gouache, watercolours.

## Materials for painting

Cartridge or brushwork paper, sketchbooks, three or four types of brush (thick (e.g. bristle), thin, chisel, soft sable), clean mixing palette or substitute thick paper, the double primary system of paints, and examples of other kinds of paint such as acrylic or watercolour, tissues or cloth for wiping brushes, sturdy water pots (keep water clean!).

# Brushmarks

▶ Look at the range of brushes. Show the children how they can hold a brush in different ways: gripping it tightly, holding it at the end, half way down, loosely, like a palette knife with thumb supporting the bristles.

▶ Talk about how to create different marks by working quickly or slowly, using the brush in different directions, pressing hard or gently, using the top, side or edge of the brush, rolling or splaying the bristles and working it wet or dry.

▶ Ask the children to choose two contrasting brushes and experiment on a sheet of white brushwork paper, to make as many different marks as they can. The experiments are endless and the children should end up with an exciting sheet of varied marks that will give them a 'visual vocabulary' when they move on to make their final painting.

# Colour mixing

▶ Help the children to discover how many colours can be made from the three primaries: red, blue and yellow. Demonstrate how to mix paint to a good consistency. Scoop a good amount of paint into a palette. Add just a few drops of water and mix to a paste before adding more water. Use a firm bristle brush, stirring carefully. Wipe the brush to avoid the water getting dirty too soon. Provide children with paper or a cloth on which to wipe the brush while they are painting.

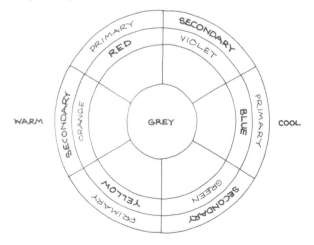

▶ Ask the children to work mathematically, mixing the three primary colours two by two to make a secondary colour and experimenting to see how many colours they can make by mixing different amounts of each of the three primaries, for example red and yellow (even amounts, more red, more yellow), then different amounts of blue in combination with each of the other two primaries.

▶ Suggest that the children keep a record of how they mixed each colour, and talk about the range of colours made.

## Tints and shades

▶ The children can continue to experiment with paint mixing. Mixing secondary colours will give more subtle colours, with a further range of different greens or browns.

These colours can all be extended by adding white to make tints or gradually adding black to make shades. Ask the children to keep a continuous record of the colours they have mixed in their sketchbooks, hypothesising and predicting as a scientist.

## Textured paint

▶ The children can experiment to see how transparent or thin the paint can be made by gradually adding more water create a wash. By contrast, they could add PVA glue or paste to see how thick the paint can become. Painting using thick paint is called *impasto*. Because of the sticky quality of the paint, pigments such as sand, earth and other powder colours can be mixed into the surface.

In the programme we see the artist mixing complementary colours. These sit opposite each other on the colour wheel. The complementary colours are made by mixing the two remaining primary colours. For example the opposite colour to red is green – made by mixing yellow and blue together.

## Still life painting

In the programme we saw the artist exploring colour mixing to make a painting of flowers. Now, having explored and experimented, the children are ready to start a still-life project.

**Step 1** Organise the children into groups. Put a vase of brightly coloured flowers on each table. (If possible, the vase and the flowers should be complementary colours.) Ask the children to organise their painting tools and materials, and remind them about their earlier experiments with colour mixing. If they are working flat on the table, they could work with one flower laid flat beside them.

**Step 2** Talk about the most appropriate way round for the paper, whether portrait or landscape. Demonstrate how to plan the painting by lightly mapping out where the vase and flowers will go using a paintbrush and light-coloured paint (it is not a good idea to use pencil). The children need to decide on the colours and mix them up, starting with the lighter colours.

Encourage the children to build up the background colour as they are painting the flowers by using the remainder of the paint on the brush just around the outside edge of the flower.

**Step 3** Remind the class not to put in too much detail too soon, to work in light colours and gradually build these up. Most importantly, remind them to step back from their work every so often to see how it is coming together.

## The language of colour

▶ Ask the childen to invent a paint-and-colour story, an abstract composition using brush marks, direction, size, speed and shapes. An example of a dictated story might be: 'Big red circles, falling from the top of the paper, meet thin green lines swirling up from the centre. They meet in the corner and dance around, gradually mixing together, and then move to the bottom of the paper, one side becoming yellow, the other turning into thick blobs of paint.'

▶ Give out the **sketchbook activity** about colour on page 11 for the children to complete.

# Sketchbook activity

▶ Make a collection of different reds using scrap paper, material, threads, sweet wrappers, flower petals, colour pencils or paints. Now stick them onto a page in your sketchbook.

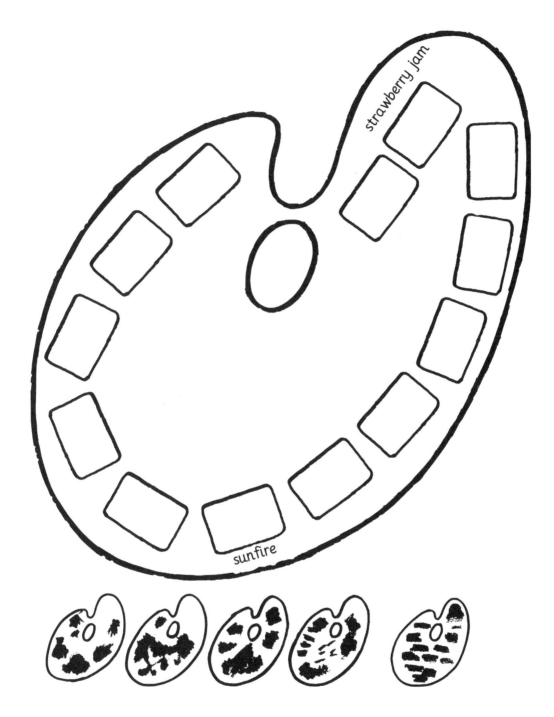

▶ Give each of the colours in your red collection a weird name, for example 'sunfire' or 'strawberry jam'.

▶ Now make another collection in a different colour. This time, when you stick them in your sketchbook, arrange them in order from light to dark.

# 3 | Pattern

## Programme outline

We visit a seaside town to look at pattern: the patterns on shells, fabrics and tiles, the patterns created by repetitive structures, the patterns of animal skins. The presenter demonstrates how to collect and develop patterns in her sketchbook and talks about the variety she finds: abstract patterns, regular and irregular patterns. We look at similar and contrasting patterns and how patterns are used to attract attention or make something blend in. We examine pattern motifs and natural geometric structures. We also look at how pattern is created: for example, is it printed on the surface of an object, or does it come from the structure itself?

The presenter takes us through the process of printing on fabric, giving detailed information on designing a pattern, how to make relief printing blocks and prepare the fabric. A class of children makes a printed wall-hanging based on the theme of the seaside.

Works of other artists include a printed silk *Ice Skaters* by Raoul Dufy, Adinkra textiles from Africa and a block-printed cotton Ajrak from Pakistan.

## Learning outcomes

The children should gain an understanding of:

- Patterns in the natural and made world.

- Using sketchbooks to collect patterns and develop design ideas.

- How patterns are created.

- Experimenting with patterns.

- Sequence in repeat patterns.

- How to organise tools, materials and equipment.

- How artists use patterns to develop designs and abstract work.

- Appropriate pattern vocabulary.

## Key concepts...

Natural and made patterns, repetition, symmetry, regular, irregular.

## ...and vocabulary

Names for different kinds of pattern, for example stripes, spots, honeycomb, spirals, geometric shapes (triangles, squares, semi-circles, hexagons), decorative, mosaics, simple, complex, abstract, motif, symbol, overlap, tessellate, print, stamp, pressure, impression, sequence, positive, negative.

## Before viewing

▶ Talk to the class about patterns and look at examples.

▶ Make a display of 'pattern' vocabulary in the classroom.

## Helpful resources: relating to pattern

Collect interesting natural objects or seaside items such as seaweed, pebbles, shells, rocks. Include contrasting 'made' seaside items such as sunglasses, plastic balls etc.

- Viewfinders, magnifying glasses, examples of printing on paper and material, a folder of examples of patterns, a display of patterns, natural, made and found objects.

## Whilst viewing

▶ The children could be asked to:

- Talk about the difference between regular and irregular shapes.

- Talk about the different places the artist finds patterns.

- Note how the artist uses her sketchbook. How does she hold the book? How far away from the subject does she stand? How does she use her pencil? What does she put on the sketchbook page?

# After viewing

Plan a printed project based on pattern-making.

▶ The class could choose to make individual prints or a larger group piece such as a hanging like the one in the programme. A whole-class textile hanging will need to be organised so that each part of the process is built up in a sequence. Plan each stage carefully. Talk about the aims of the project with the class to develop the children's knowledge, understanding and skills in pattern-making and printing.

## Materials and equipment for printing

Printing blocks (pieces of off-cut wood can be bought cheaply from a wood yard), inking tray, printing ink or paint, glue and spreaders, string, scraps of wood and card to stick on blocks, printing paper, fabric to print on, masking tape, rags and overalls, newspaper for cushioning and blotting prints.

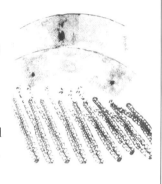

*Hint:* Inking trays will remain usable for several lessons if wrapped up well in a plastic bag at the end of each session.

## Organisation

▶ Look at the tools and materials needed to make a print and discuss with the class how to organise the printing area. Prints take time to dry. Blotting helps, but plan the drying space, if possible, allowing a day for the prints to dry. Watch for draughts so that wet prints do not stick together and allow plenty of time for clearing up. Remind the children to keep their hands clean. If possible, separate out the activities into three areas: preparing the block, inking the block and taking the impression from the printing block.

## Looking for patterns

▶ The children can use their sketchbooks to collect and record patterns found in the classroom, school or local environment. Remind the children to use the pages of their sketchbook well and draw or collect as much information as possible.

▶ After brainstorming ideas on a chosen theme such as sport or the seaside, ask the class to make sketches of objects relating to the theme.

From their drawings, they can select an object with an interesting, bold outline shape.

## Printing blocks

▶ Ask the children to draw their shape on thin sponge, or card, making it smaller than the size of the block. Stick the cut-out shape onto the block using strong glue. Allow the blocks to dry overnight.

Alternatively, printing blocks can be made using sticking string, card off-cuts or artstraws.

Plasticine prints can also provide a quick and effective stamp. Ask the children to roll a softened piece of Plasticine in their hand and pull it into a point to make a 'handle' on one side. Because the Plasticine is soft, objects can be pressed hard into it leaving an impression that can be inked and printed.

String can be tricky. It is best to cover the top of the block with glue and drop the string onto it, arranging it with a pencil rather than with fingers. Remind the children that any motif will print in reverse.

## The printing

▶ The print block can print onto paper to make a wallpaper or wrapping-paper design. For printing on fabric, a soft-covered table-top or floor with a thick layer of newspaper will be needed. Cotton material is best to print on (an old bed sheet or other material that is non-starch). Stretch the fabric tightly over the table and tape it down so that it is smooth and not creased. Try printing on prepared backgrounds made by painting a wash over the material or paper, or sponging the material with dyes, before beginning to print the relief blocks over the top.

**Step 1**  Use printing ink rather than paint. If the print is to be a hanging or a design that will be washed, use textile ink or ink that can be fixed. Squeeze a little of the ink onto an inking tray and gently spread it using a roller so that it is even. If the ink is too thick it will fill in any open parts on the block and print unevenly. Listen for the tacky sound the roller makes on the ink. Depending on how complicated the motif is, the children can either press the block into the ink to cover it or use a roller and roll it onto the motif, making sure the area of the motif is well covered.

**Step 2**  Get the children to test out their prints on a scrap of paper. They can think about possible alternative ways to create the pattern before moving on to the material itself. Talk about the best colour scheme for the hanging, and decide how many colours to use. Often pattern designs work best when they are limited o a few colours only.

**Step 3**  Decide with the children whether to start printing in the middle and work outwards, to work from the left to the right hand side, or to make a border around the edge. They also need to work out how many motifs will fit in the length of material. The final piece could be based on a regular pattern or have more randomly placed motifs.

**Step 4**  Decide with the class whether they will take it in turns to make their impression. If working from the middle outwards, the taller children may need to print first. Make sure they keep an even pressure, pressing down on the material without moving the block. The group will need to take turns and work co-operatively. If printing each block in a different colour, it is helpful to work from light to dark.

**Step 5**  When the final print has been made, display the hanging and ask the class for their opinions.

## Developing patterns

Patterns are made by repeating a motif across a surface. Bands of patterns can be created using a very simple motif and experimenting with it in various ways. This is what the **sketchbook activity** on page 15 asks the children to do. The motif can be a drawn shape or a cut-out paper shape (these could be photocopied for the children and cut out). A repeating a motif can also be produced quickly and effectively using an IT art program.

## Pattern collections

▶  Each of these could be a sketchbook activity.

**Patterns across the world**  Exciting patterns can be found across the world. Ask the children to research and collect examples, such as the Mehndi hand designs of India and Pakistan or the traditional Ghanaian Adinkra cloth symbols, printed with a carved calabash shell.

**Patterns in history**  There are many more patterns to be found in history. Greek, Egyptian, Elizabethan, Tudor and Roman mosaic designs can all form an interesting collection for sketchbook work.

**Patterns in mathematics**  There will be many opportunities to focus on the vocabulary of mathematics to develop pattern work using tessellation, translation, rotation, measurement, size, proportion and prediction.

**Patterns in paintings**  Patterns can be found in the paintings of artists such as Gustav Klimt, Matisse and Eduard Vuillard. Ask the children to find the pattern using a viewfinder and magnifying glass, and to recreate it, trying hard to match the colours as well as the lines and shapes.

## The language of pattern

▶  Make patterns with words and letters – as in handwriting. This activity could be extended using palindromic words such as *tot, gag, nun*.

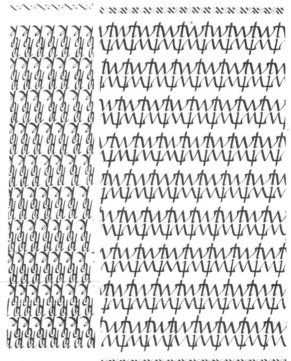

# Sketchbook activity

▶ Here are some patterns made from a shell motif. Cut them out and stick them in your sketchbook. Write the kind of pattern underneath. Choose from this list:

- place in a row
- turn in alternate directions
- leave a space between each motif
- use only half of the motif

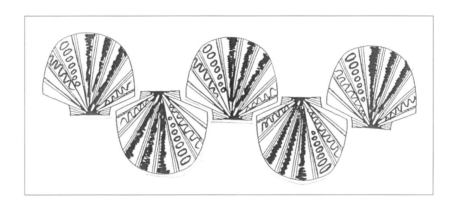

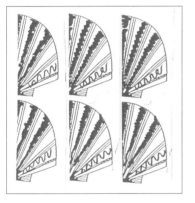

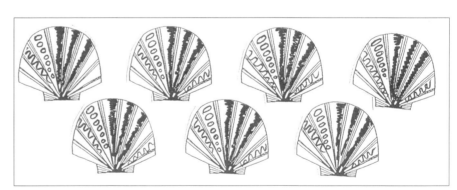

▶ Now find a shell and draw it in your sketchbook. Look closely at the textures and shapes.

▶ Use a viewfinder to choose an interesting part of your drawing. With a hard pencil (HB), trace it. Include the edge of the viewfinder as well.

▶ Now you can use your traced motif to make another pattern.

# Texture

## Programme outline

Two different environments, a home and a garden, present a range of textures both natural and manufactured. Inside the home, various materials are explored: wood, metal, brick, glass, fabric. The presenter makes rubbings of textured surfaces and experiments with drawing different textures in her sketchbook. In the kitchen are lots of smooth, flat, hard surfaces. The bedroom, by contrast, uses much softer materials. Outside in the garden the textures are different again. The descriptive words used, for example 'smooth', 'spiky', 'grainy', 'soft', 'fluffy', 'corrugated', give a sense of how different textures feel.

Back in the studio, the presenter demonstrates different ways to create texture: mixing paint with glue and other materials; using different brushes, sponges, newspapers, combs; using paint techniques such as colour washing and tonking. She makes a picture collage of textures found in a home by combining paint and other materials.

The work of other artists includes that of British artist Gillian Ayres, American artist Tom Wesselmann's *Bathroom Collage,* and Elizabeth Blackadder's still life *Bamboo and Gold.*

## Learning outcomes

The children should gain an understanding of:

- Visual, tactile and sensory elements in the natural and made worlds.

- Making textures in a variety of ways.

- The qualities of different materials, for example wood, metal, plastic.

- How artists, sculptors and designers use textures in their work.

- Appropriate vocabulary related to texture.

- Selecting and using materials in making collages.

## Key concepts...

Abstract, realistic, sensory, relief, raised surface, impression, scrunch, scrape, sgrafitto, impasto, rubbings, collage.

## ...and vocabulary

Adjectives, for example smooth, jagged, bristly, soft, rough, gritty. Materials, for example stone, wood, bark, leather, plastic, glass, china, rubber, polythene, corrugated card, moss, grass, hair, material, velvet, silk, muslin, hessian, fur, felt, lace. Different kinds of paper, for example tissue, crêpe, cellophane.

## Before viewing

▶ Play a 'feely bag' game by putting different textured objects in a non-see-through bag. Ask the children to close their eyes, feel inside the bag and describe what the textures feel like. Use their words to begin a texture word list which can be developed later in sketchbooks.

▶ Use a thick wax crayon (on its side) and a sheet of newsprint paper to make rubbings of objects inside the classroom or on the school grounds.

▶ Explore mark-making with felt pens or crayons or use an IT art program to create textural effects.

▶ As a class, talk about the room you are in and all the textures represented in it. Ask the children to list the items and surfaces and their materials. Then, by the side of these, add a word which best describes the texture.

## Helpful resources: for texture

Collect a wide range of materials: a texture box, viewfinders, magnifying glasses, Braille (examples can be found on cleaning products).

- A collection of natural and made objects.

- A display about textures which pupils can add to.

- Pictures of artists' and sculptors' work showing an emphasis on texture.

# Whilst viewing

▶ The children could be asked to:

- Record some of the textures shown in the programme in their sketchbooks.

- Speak about the difference between seen and felt textures.

# After viewing

## Planning a texture collage

▶ On a theme of 'my house' or 'our school', ask the children to make a collage to show the different aspects of texture. Talk about the aims of the project which are to develop the children's knowledge and understanding of texture and skills in collage work. Introduce the project by looking at examples of texture and talking about what texture is and where it can be found. Emphasise that much of the work will be about exploring and experimenting with texture as well as making a collage.

▶ Give out the **sketchbook activity** on page 19 and ask the children to complete it. Remind them what they learnt about line and tone.

## Materials and equipment

Glue and spreaders, scraps of wood, material, card, threads, a range of different kinds of paper (e.g. tissue, crêpe, tracing paper, sketchbooks, A3 or A2 paper or thin card), paint thickened with PVA glue, card combs, stiff brushes (to push paint onto the surface rather than paint it as in a wash), scissors.

## Further ideas

Textures can also be explored by:

- Pencil and wax rubbings on paper.

- Pressing objects into clay to create a textured impression (these can also be printed).

- Crushing, cutting, and distressing paper in a variety of ways.

- Using thick paint (powder paint with PVA glue added) and adding sand or earth.

- Covering a surface with thick paint and scratching into it with different tools such as a card comb (a small piece of card with teeth cut into it).

- Drawing and mark-making using large felt pens and wax crayons.

- Using wax crayons with a wash of diluted paint or ink over the top (a resist technique).

## Mark-making tools

▶ Show the class how to make their own mark-making tools, for example a brush made with sticks of wood with twigs, pipe cleaners, wool, sponge or raffia tied to the top. Other 'found' tools such as old decorating brushes, scrubbing brushes, tooth brushes and scouring pads can also make interesting and exciting textural effects.

## Making textured effects

▶ Prepare a large tray of paint (one colour is best and black emphasises the textures well). Children can dip the 'made' tools into the tray of paint and investigate the different marks that can be made on large sheets of paper. They should try moving their mark-making

tools in different directions and at different speeds. When the class have created several sheets of textures, allow them to dry.

▶ Talk about which of the tools were responsible for which of the effects and find out what the children think of them. These sheets can be used to develop a collage. Share the textured sheets amongst the class. Ask them to tear, rather than cut, small pieces of different textures and, overlapping them slightly, stick them onto a picture. Each of the textured sections will be placed in a different space.

This activity is also a helpful way to explore the concept of distance in landscape work, where dark, bold texture marks are used in the foreground with lighter, smaller marks in the distance.

## A texture collage

**Step 1** Ask the children to choose how many rooms they will have in their collage house and make a cross-section drawing of the inside. The number of sections will depend on the number of rooms. They might also draw a bird's-eye view of a garden, dividing it into sections to represent different textures.

**Step 2** Suggest that the children make a list on their drawing of all the items that they would find in each room together with adjectives that describe their textures. Each room would be different.

**Step 3** Organise the class so that the activities of cutting and gluing are separated. Ask the children to divide their table space into two halves so that the cutting, tearing and collecting of textured pieces is on one side of the table and the gluing on the other.

*Hint:* Suggest that they use spreaders for glue, not brushes, and that they don't glue in the air. They can either glue the piece laid flat on the table or glue the area on the picture and press the cut piece onto it.

The class could be divided into groups with each one doing a different room. The individual rooms would then become a composite 'house'.

**Step 4** The children can now prepare the background made on paper. This could be done simply using a watery paint, or more boldly with textured paint.

**Step 5** With the background prepared, the 'rooms' can be given their textural finish.

**Step 6** When complete, display the collages and ask the class to identify which room is which.

## Materials

In preparation, collect a range of textures similar to those found in the paintings, e.g. twigs, fabric, leaves, grass, food.

## The language of texture

▶ Choose a reproduction of a painting that shows strong textural qualities. For example, Henri de Sidaner's *Picnic in the Woods* features people sitting on the grass by a river having a picnic. Using reproductions is not the same as looking at the real thing, but the quality of the texture of the lines, shapes and brushstrokes can be described in words. Talk with the class about how these textures might feel if they could touch them.

Place the painting in the middle of a large sheet of paper. Encourage the children to imagine they are in the middle of the painting, and ask the following questions:

- What sounds do you think you would you hear?

- What do you think the conversation of the people would be? (This could be developed as a role play.)

- What do you think you would you smell? Does it remind you of anything?

▶ The children can recreate the painting by making their own abstract textural collage.

# Sketchbook activity

▶ In your sketchbook make marks using a pencil to show:

- a soft texture

- a shiny texture

- a hard texture

- a spiky texture

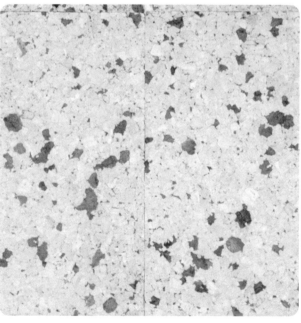

▶ Now draw four things in your sketchbook that you might find at home. Show how each of these would feel if you touched them by making marks which show their texture.

# 5 | Structure

## Programme outline

The programme is set in a market which provides a starting point for an investigation of three-dimensional shapes. The natures of two- and three-dimensional shapes are explored using a piece of fruit. In the street more shapes are found that represent cubes, spheres and cylinders. These basic shapes are drawn by the presenter in her sketchbook. She divides the page into four to show different views of each object. In modelling work, a basic understanding of structure is very helpful. She uses the example of a building to reinforce this point.

However, the shape of the fruit in the market is not regular. But it still needs a skeleton to make it stand up on its own. Understanding the basic structure of an object, for example that a banana is a tube with a bend in the middle, helps when it comes to three-dimensional work. Back in the studio the presenter demonstrates 3-D modelling techniques. Using withy cane and tissue paper, she shows us how to make a giant pineapple sculpture. Three groups of children are seen working on different models of fruit.

Finally, other artists who make three-dimensional sculptures include David Mach, Ellis O'Connell and David Nash.

## Learning outcomes

The children should gain an understanding of:

- Visual and tactile sensations.

- Structure, texture, shape, form, space, scale, size, dimension and proportion.

- Using a sketchbook to record from observation and to plan ideas.

- Manipulative skills using a variety of materials, tools and equipment.

- How to adapt and modify work as it develops, and how to solve problems.

- Working co-operatively, with organisation and safety.

- Three-dimensional work in the environment.

- Vocabulary related to structure, form and space.

## Key concepts...

Regular, irregular, tactile, shape, form, space, size, texture, dimension, proportion, three-dimensional drawing.

## ...and vocabulary

Sphere, cone, cylinder, cube, pyramid, structure, balance, frame, skeleton, scale, inside, outside, additive, subtractive, manipulate. Names and properties of different materials: wood, clay, plastics, wire, card, papers, stone, granite, steel, marble, bronze. Recycled and reclaimed materials. Imagination, evaluating, problem solving. Properties and limitations of materials: malleable, rigid.

## Before viewing

▶ Ask the children to describe shapes and forms in the classroom. Talk about the fact that three-dimensional work can be walked around or handled and looked at from many viewpoints. Some three-dimensional works are a solid mass while others contain space and use rods, canes, wire or sticks to create a skeleton frame. The 'space' within the sculpture is important. Some sculpture is a combination of both – a solid form with rounded holes and shapes cut from it (Barbara Hepworth and Henry Moore).

Working with three-dimensional objects, especially found items, can develop imagination. A piece of driftwood can become a strange creature. Picasso imagined bicycle handlebars to be like a bull's head and often had great fun turning found objects into something else in his sculptures.

Three-dimensional structures can be made:

- by an 'additive' method where materials such as clay, Plasticine, salt dough, found materials, wood, card, paper, wire or plaster are built up, joined together, added to and constructed, modelled or moulded;

- by a 'subtractive' method where materials such as clay, plaster, soap, polystyrene and wood are cut into or carved away.

## Helpful resources: for sculpture

Make a collection of three-dimensional objects such as vases, pots, ornaments, puppets, toys, items used for worship or celebration, items used for a practical purpose, such as a cooking pot, and items that are purely for decoration.

Collect examples of the work of sculptors made from a wide range of materials. Label them under categories such as: three-dimensional figures, animals, birds, sculpture and relief work across the world, abstract three-dimensional contemporary sculptures, land sculptures, monumental sculptures seen in parks and cities.

- Information about sculpture parks and sculptures in your location, storage boxes of an accessible height used for categorising different kinds of material and card, tubes, boxes and threads.

## Moving from two to three dimensions

▶ To introduce the children to the concept of a flat surface becoming three-dimensional, use a simple activity. Cut a small square of card. Ask the children to cut this into three equal pieces. Cut slots in them and push them together so that the slots interlock. This will give a structure that can stand up.

A number of alternative structures can be made by re-slotting or adding cut shapes. Talk about the shapes and the strengths and weaknesses of the structure.

# Whilst viewing

▶ The children could be asked:

- To describe some of the shapes and forms seen in the programme.

- How the presenter draws shapes in her sketchbook.

- What difference the size of a sculpture makes.

- To talk about the kinds of fruit seen in the programme: where they come from and how they taste.

# After viewing
## Plan a sculpture project with the class

▶ Remind the children about working in three dimensions: the aims, the organisation and safety, and the need for concentration, on-going discussion, modification and co-operation. Emphasise that there are no right or wrong approaches. A 3-D project is best planned over a period of time to allow for drying.

▶ Demonstrate the skills of cutting, gluing, joining and modelling, and allow the children time to experiment to develop these. You could use either the withy structure method, as in the programme, or clay, to make a whole-class three-dimensional bowl of fruit.

## Make a bowl of large fruit: using withy

▶ Working on a large scale will require withies. (Small-scale work can be done with long pipe cleaners or soft wire.) Plan with the children the space needed to store the models while working on them. Investigating the structure and space, make a frame or skeleton of the fruit.

### Preparation using sketchbooks

▶ Ask the children to investigate the fruits of the Caribbean. In their sketchbooks, ask them to divide a page and to draw the fruit from four different viewpoints, using lines to show the outlines and shading to show the forms. Talk about the scale, dimensions, proportions and texture of the fruit. Ask the children to cut their fruit in halves or quarters and to make drawings of the patterns and textures inside.

## Materials for withy work

A bundle of withies (dampened to make them more flexible), scissors, string, masking tape (torn into small lengths), glue and water mix, newspaper, white tissue paper (to allow maximum light in the structure), a bowl, rags, plastic table-top covering.

*Hint:* There are no hard-and-fast rules about working with withy. It takes practice to discover how it bends and it is necessary to experiment with the sorts of shapes to which it lends itself. Tear small bits of masking tape and hang them on the edge of table for easy access. Tape each joint securely.

Organisation

Organise the children in pairs or small groups. Start with a simple shape. Allow a good working area and cover the floor or table area with a plastic sheet.

**Making a withy construction**

**Step 1** Practise bending and taping the withies with the children. Decide on the shape and size and how many strips of withy will be needed. Bend the withy gently into the main shape and tape with masking tape where the ends meet. Start with the outline and use the heavier ends of the withies on the area of least curvature and greatest strength.

**Step 2** Add the skin to the frame using tissue paper. The children should use a sponge, dipped into a bowl of glue and water mix, to cover a sheet of tissue paper, without getting it so wet that it tears.

**Step 3** In pairs, the children will need to lay the tissue carefully over the withy shape. The tissue edge should be built up round the withy and pulled gently to tighten. It will tighten as it dries and any creases will add interest. When dry it should be coated with a watered-down PVA glue mixture to harden.

**Step 4** You can use paint, tissue or dyes to colour it. You may even want to attach threads of colour.

# Make a bowl of fruit: using clay

▶ Ask the children to make small, solid models of their fruit in clay or other modelling material. Find some examples of clay objects. Before beginning, spend some time talking about clay. What is it? Where do we find it? What does it feel like? Talk about how it changes from a wet, malleable medium to a 'fired' hard object. Look at clay work that has been modelled: a hand-built pot and a machine-made, mass-produced item.

## Materials for clay

Clay and clay tools, newspaper, rolling pins, hessian, sponges and rags (specially kept for clay work), boards, card or wood, polythene bags, overalls.

*Hint:* It is important to keep the clay workable – not too dry and not too wet. Wrap up work at the end of each lesson.

**Exploring clay**

**Step 1** Take a hand-sized ball of clay. Ask the children to handle it, to poke, pull, push, pinch, and prod it using different parts of their fingers and hands. Practise rolling coils and pushing things into a flattened piece of clay to create a texture. Join pieces of clay together with 'slip' – a very watery version of the clay.

**Step 2** Make a small model of a section of fruit. Show how to make a pinch pot. Make a small ball of clay in your hand. Press your thumb downwards into the centre of the clay and squeeze it, gently flattening and pulling the sides towards your thumb. Turn the ball of clay in the palm of your hand until you have a small bowl shape.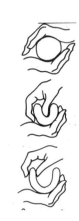

**Step 3** Encourage the children to use this as the 'basic shape' for the fruit and gradually build an interesting structure by adding small coils of clay or pressing textures into the surfaces.

**Step 4** Two pinch pots pushed together will form a basic sphere shape. This can be built on with coils of clay to become all manner of fruit forms.

**Step 5** When the clay model is finished, allow it to dry. The final piece can be fired in a kiln or – as with 'new' clay – air-hardened.

**Step 6** The children can now decorate their fruit with paints (PVA glue added to the paint will strengthen it) or glazes.

# The language of sculpture

▶ The **sketchbook activity** on page 23 asks the children to talk about the materials that the sculptures on the page might be made from and how they might feel if touched. Give this sheet out for them to work on and get them to record their answers in their sketchbook.

# Sketchbook activity

Here is a picture of an abstract sculpture.

▶ Look at it carefully and then make a drawing of it in your sketchbook. If you like, you can cut it out and stick it into your sketchbook next to your drawing.

▶ Now use your imagination to write a story about it. These questions will help you:

• What is it? Is it a head, a machine, a creature from another planet?

• If you were standing next to it, how big might it be?

• What sound might it make?

• If it came to life how might it move?

• Where might it have come from?

• What sort of public place would you put it in?

# Further information

## Art Galleries

Aberdeen – **Art Gallery**  Tel: 01224 646333

Bath – **Victoria Art Gallery**  Tel: 01225 352124

Birmingham – **City Museum & Art Gallery**
Tel: 0121 235 2834

Bradford – **The Colour Museum**  Tel: 01274 390955

Bristol
**Arnolfini**  Tel: 0117 929 9191
**City Museum & Art Gallery**  Tel: 0117 922 3571

Cambridge – **Fitzwilliam Gallery**  Tel: 01223 332993

Cardiff – **National Art Gallery**  Tel: 01222 397951

Eastbourne – **Towner Art Gallery**  Tel: 01323 725112

Glasgow – **Museum**  Tel: 0141 357 3929

Leeds – **City Art Gallery**  Tel: 0113 2478264

Leicester – **Museum of Costume**  Tel: 0116 247 3056

Liverpool – **Tate Gallery**  Tel: 0151 709 3223

London
**Commonwealth Institute**  Tel: 0171 603 4535
**Courtauld Institute**  Tel: 0171 873 2620
**Dulwich Picture Gallery**  Tel: 0181 693 6911
**Imperial War Museum**  Tel: 0171 416 5000
**Museum of Mankind**  Tel: 0171 636 1555
**National Gallery**  Tel: 0171 839 3321
**National Portrait Gallery**  Tel: 0171 306 0055
**Tate Gallery**  Tel: 0171 887 8000
**Victoria & Albert Museum**  Tel: 0171 938 8500

Manchester – **City Art Gallery**  Tel: 0161 236 5244

Oxford
**Ashmolean**  Tel: 01865 278000
**Museum of Modern Art**  Tel: 01865 722733

Powys – **Museum of Modern Art**  Tel: 01654 703355

St Albans – **City Museum**  Tel: 01727 819339

St Ives – **Tate Gallery**  Tel: 01736 796545

Sheffield – **Mappin Gallery**  Tel: 0114 272 6281

Southampton – **City Art Gallery**  Tel: 01703 223855

Tenby – **Museum & Picture Gallery**
Tel: 01834 842809

## Books

*Approaches to Art,* Anthea Peppin & Ray Smith. Ginn 1993

*What is Art?,* Rosemary Dickinson. OUP

*A Teacher's Guide to Learning from Objects,* G Durbin, S Morris & G Wilkinson. English Heritage

*Sketchbooks: Explore and Store,* Gillian Robinson. Hodder & Stoughton

*Understanding Modern Art,* Monica Bohm-Duchen & Janet Cook. Usborne

*Themes in Art for Ages 7 –11.* Thames & Hudson.

*Masquerade: Schemes of Work for Art in the Primary School,* Judy Cam, Ruth Elia & Trilby Lawlor. Available from the Visual Learning Foundation, Robert Blair School, Brewery Road, Islington, London N7 9QJ. Tel: 0171 609 7155.

## Materials

**Withy suppliers**

J. Burdekin Ltd, 172 Wakefield Road, Ossett, Wakefield, W. Yorks. WF5 9AQ

**Paint**

The 'double primary system' of paint consists of a warm and cool for each of the primary colours: warm and cool red, warm and cool blue, and warm and cool yellow. With the addition of white, children should be able to mix most colours from this range. Acrylic ready-mix paint is available from:

Thomas Seth, Holly House, Castle Hill, Hartley, Kent DA3 7BH

**Sculpture**

Galvanised wire is available from any local hardware shop. Aluminium armature wire (0.3mm) for larger sculptures may be purchased from specialist sculpture material suppliers.

Alec Tiranti Ltd, 27 Warren Street, London W1P 5DG